CORE WRITING SKILLS

How to Write an Explanatory Text

Sara Howell

PowerKiDS press.

New York

Published in 2014 by The Rosen Publishing Group, Inc.
29 East 21st Street, New York, NY 10010

First Edition

Editor: Amelie von Zumbusch
Book Design: Andrew Povolny
Photo Research: Katie Stryker

Photo Credits: Cover KidStock/Blend Images/Getty Images; p. 5 Muellek Josef/Shutterstock.com; p. 6 Domenic Gareri/Shutterstock.com; p. 8 Kavram/Shutterstock.com; p. 10 Lisa F. Young/Shutterstock.com; p. 11 Jacek Chabraszewski/Shutterstock.com; p. 12 mlorenz/Shutterstock.com; p. 13 photobank.kiev.ua/Shutterstock.com; p. 16 Rob Marmion/Shutterstock.com; p. 19 Monkey Business Images/Shutterstock.com; p. 20 Jose Luis Pelaez Inc/Blend Images/Getty Images; p. 21 Naypong/Shutterstock.com; p. 22 Jorg Hackemann/Shutterstock.com.

Publisher's Cataloging Data

Howell, Sara.
How to write an explanatory text / by Sara Howell.
  p. cm. — (Core writing skills)
Includes index.
ISBN 978-1-4777-2907-6 (library binding) — ISBN 978-1-4777-2996-0 (pbk.) — ISBN 978-1-4777-3066-9 (6-pack)
1. English language — Composition and exercises — Juvenile literature. I. Howell, Sara. II. Title.
PE1408.H69 2014
808—d23

Manufactured in the United States of America

CPSIA Compliance Information: Batch #W14PK4: For Further Information contact Rosen Publishing, New York, New York at 1-800-237-9932

CONTENTS

WHAT IS AN EXPLANATORY TEXT?

Suppose a friend asked you how soccer is played. What would you tell her? You might start by explaining that soccer is played with a ball. You could tell her about different player positions and how points are scored. You could finish by explaining that the team with the most points wins.

Writing an explanatory text is a lot like answering this sort of question. Explanatory texts give information about **topics**. In school, your teacher might ask you to explain how clouds form or why the American Revolution was fought. A good explanatory text examines a topic and conveys ideas and information clearly.

Writing Tip

If you have a choice, pick a writing topic that interests you and that you would like to learn more about.

Explanatory texts are a great way to learn more about topics that interest you, from parrots to paintball to Parmesan cheese!

It is important to let readers know what your explanatory text is about right away. This helps them decide if it is something they would like to read. You should **introduce**, or present, your topic in the first few sentences. This first **paragraph**, or section, of your piece is called the introduction.

If you are writing an explanatory text about a famous person, explain what that person is famous for in your introduction.

The bald eagle is the national bird of the United States. It lives only in North America. It nearly died out in the mid-twentieth century but has since made a comeback.

Interesting opening fact

Basic supporting facts

The introduction is also your chance to get readers interested. Including a fun fact about your topic is a great way to do that. In a piece about how ice cream is made, you might begin by saying that each American eats nearly 6 gallons (23 l) of ice cream every year!

Writing Tip

A good, clear title is important. Try writing your title as a question, then make sure your piece really answers that question.

FACTS, DEFINITIONS, AND DETAILS

The body of your piece gives readers information, or facts. Facts are statements that can be proven. "Poodles are the best pets" is not a fact. Someone else may think goldfish make the best pets. Neither idea can be proven right or wrong. "Poodles are a kind of dog," though, is a fact.

Writing Tip

Explanatory texts are often written in the present tense, or as if they are happening right now.

Flash floods helped shape Antelope Canyon. If you were writing about the canyon, you might explain that flash floods are very sudden floods in low-lying areas.

CHART OF FACTS AND OPINIONS

OPINIONS	FACTS
CHERRIES ARE DELICIOUS.	CHERRIES GROW ON TREES.
BRAVE IS A GREAT MOVIE.	BRAVE IS SET IN SCOTLAND.
PANDAS ARE THE CUTEST ANIMALS.	PANDAS COME FROM CHINA.
YOSEMITE NATIONAL PARK IS TOO CROWDED.	YOSEMITE NATIONAL PARK IS IN CALIFORNIA.

Details, or extra facts, give even more information. If you write, "poodles come in three sizes," a good detail might be that those sizes are called standard, miniature, and toy. If you use words that might be unfamiliar to your readers, include **definitions** to explain what those words mean.

READY FOR RESEARCH

There are probably some topics that you already know a lot about. Others, however, will be unfamiliar. To write an explanatory text about an unfamiliar topic, you will need to **research**, or study, the topic and gather information.

If you are not sure where to start your research, ask a librarian! Librarians know a lot about research.

Your library may have several books on the topic you are researching. Look at each of them and pick the ones that seem most useful.

Writing Tip

Use a dictionary to find definitions of words you do not understand. Include those definitions in your piece for readers.

The best way to begin your research will often depend on the topic. If you are writing about reptiles, an **encyclopedia** or a website run by a zoo would be good places to start. If you are writing about your grandfather, though, your best **sources** of information would likely be members of your family.

GROUPING INFORMATION

Before you begin writing, **organize** your information. Look for facts that have some kind of connection. For example, if you were researching the state of Florida, you would learn that more than 19 million people live there. You would learn that the Florida city with the most people is Jacksonville and that most of the oranges sold in the United States are grown there.

If you are writing an explanatory text about moose, you might want to put all the facts about what they eat in one paragraph.

Writing Tip

Try writing each fact on its own index card. Move the cards around in different groups until everything makes sense.

These first two facts are both related to the state's population. They can be grouped together in one paragraph. The third fact has to do with the types of crops grown in Florida and would fit best in a different paragraph.

Decide how you are going to organize your facts before you start writing your explanatory text.

Have you ever heard someone say a picture is worth a thousand words? Illustrations are a great way to help explain and examine your topic. They can even help you organize your information before you start writing. Try using maps, graphs, charts, and **diagrams** in your piece to aid readers' comprehension, or understanding.

BOBCAT RANGE MAP

A range map shows where a kind of animal lives.

KEY

WHERE BOBCATS LIVE

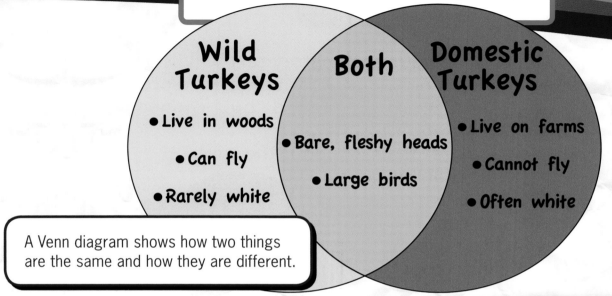

Venn Diagram Comparing Kinds of Turkeys

Wild Turkeys
- Live in woods
- Can fly
- Rarely white

Both
- Bare, fleshy heads
- Large birds

Domestic Turkeys
- Live on farms
- Cannot fly
- Often white

A Venn diagram shows how two things are the same and how they are different.

Choose the type of illustration or **graphic organizer** that makes the most sense for your topic. A diagram is a good way to show the water cycle or an animal's life cycle. Graphs can show changes over time. Maps are useful for showing where animals or people live.

Writing Tip

Graphs, maps, and other graphic organizers should have titles. Photos should have captions to show how they relate.

LINKING IDEAS

The body of your explanatory text will list many facts. Linking words help connect these facts. Words such as "also," "another," "more," and "but" connect ideas within groups of information.

Look again at the fact about the number of oranges grown in Florida. Linking words can connect this fact to facts about other crops grown in Florida.

Have you ever had to stay home because you were sick? The word "because" shows that the thought that follows depends on the thought that came before it.

Édouard-René Lefebvre de Laboulaye came up with the idea of the Statue of Liberty. Sculptor Frédéric-Auguste Bartholdi (also) became interested in the idea (and) began building it several years later. (Finally,) it was set up in New York Harbor in 1885.

Linking words

Writing Tip

Use linking words such as "first," "second," "then," and "finally" to show the order in which things happen.

For example, you could say that 74 percent of oranges sold in the United States are grown in Florida. Florida also grows more green beans than any other state. Strawberries are another crop grown in Florida. The words "also" and "another" here connect these facts and ideas together.

The last section of your explanatory piece is called the conclusion. This short paragraph is where you conclude, or end, your piece. You can start by writing a short **summary** of your main ideas and key details. Be careful not to repeat yourself, though. You do not need to add new information. However, you should state your information in a new, interesting way.

Use your conclusion to show readers why they should care about your topic and why it is important. A good conclusion can excite readers to start their own research and learn even more!

Writing Tip

You might find it helpful to start your conclusion with phrases such as "to sum up" or "in conclusion."

Your conclusion is a great place to make an argument for the importance of your topic.

PUT TECHNOLOGY TO WORK

Technology is all around us, from computers and tablets to email and the Internet. Did you know you can use these tools to research and write your explanatory piece and then share it with the world? Using technology may even help you become a better writer!

If you write about a topic that really interests you, you may want to start a website or blog about it.

Writing on a computer makes it easy to revise, or make changes to, your explanatory text.

If your classmates or friends write their own pieces on different topics, think about creating a website together. You might end up teaching people around the world about your topic!

If you use the Internet to share your explanatory text, friends can read it on computers, tablets, and smartphones.

21

Much of the information we learn comes from explanatory pieces, such as textbooks. Learning to write a well-organized explanatory text of your own can help you identify main ideas and connections in the texts you read.

Learning to convey ideas and information clearly in your writing is very important, too. The steps and tips in this book can help you master this skill. Writing clear and organized explanatory texts is a skill you can use for the rest of your life!

You can write explanatory texts about many topics, such as interesting people, animals, ideas, and places.

GLOSSARY

definitions (deh-feh-NIH-shenz) The meanings of words.

details (dih-TAYLZ) Extra facts.

diagrams (DY-uh-gramz) Pictures of things.

encyclopedia (in-sy-kluh-PEE-dee-uh) A book that has information about a wide range of subjects, usually in alphabetical order.

graphic organizer (GRA-fik OR-guh-ny-zer) A chart, graph, or picture that sorts facts and ideas and makes them clear.

introduce (in-truh-DOOS) To start a piece by explaining what is going to follow.

organize (OR-guh-nyz) To have things neat and in order.

paragraph (PAR-uh-graf) A group of sentences about a certain subject or idea.

research (REE-serch) To study something carefully to find out more about it.

sources (SORS-ez) Things that give facts or knowledge.

summary (SUH-muh-ree) A short account of something that has been said or written.

topics (TAH-piks) The subjects of pieces of writing.

INDEX

WEBSITES

Due to the changing nature of Internet links, PowerKids Press has developed an online list of websites related to the subject of this book. This site is updated regularly. Please use this link to access the list: www.powerkidslinks.com/cws/explan/